These are some suggestions for continuing the learning process through practical, fun activities.

Grow a sunflower

This activity will enable children to watch the changes that take place when a seed grows into a sunflower.

You will need (for each child) a few sunflower seeds, a flowerpot, compost, a tape measure.

What to do:
1. Plant a few sunflower seeds in some compost in a flowerpot. (If more than one seed germinates, additional seedlings could be transferred to other pots.)
2. Talk about the conditions that a sunflower needs to grow. Place the pot on a windowsill and ask the children to be responsible for checking that the compost does not dry out.
3. Make a chart together to note any changes and record the height of the sunflower on a weekly basis.
4. You could also try planting other seeds, for example: cress seeds, pumpkin seeds.
5. Design an experiment together to find out what happens when a seedling is deprived of water or light.

Sunflower height chart

This cross-curricular craft activity for a small group of children provides further practice with measuring.

You will need a left-over roll of wallpaper (remnant rolls are cheap; avoid ready-pasted varieties), paints, tape measure, green card, scissors, Blu-tack.

What to do:
1. Cut a length of wallpaper to at least 30 cm longer than the height of the children.
2. On the non-patterned side, use paint to draw and colour a large sunflower shape at the top of the paper.
3. Using green paint, draw a thick stem from the flower to the base of the wallpaper sheet. Add leaves along the stem.
4. Using a tape measure, mark 5 cm intervals from the base of the stem to the flower. Help the children to label the marks in centimetres, counting in fives.
5. Attach the height chart to a wall. Check that the first marked measurement - 5 cm - is positioned exactly 5 cm from the ground.
6. Cut leaves out of the green card and ask each child to write their name on one leaf. They can then stick the leaf-markers to the chart with Blu-tack, to show their height.

This edition first published in 2005

Editor   April McCroskie
Language Consultant   Prue Goodwin

An SBC Book
Conceived, edited and designed by
The Salariya Book Company
25 Marlborough Place Brighton BN1 1UB
© The Salariya Book Company Ltd MCMXCVII

Dr Gerald Legg holds a doctorate in zoology from Manchester University. His current position is biologist at the Booth Museum of Natural History in Brighton.

Carolyn Scrace is a graduate of Brighton College of Art, specialising in design and illustration. She has worked in animation, advertising and children's fiction.

Prue Goodwin is a freelance educational consultant and lecturer at the National Centre for Language and Literacy in Reading.

David Salariya was born in Dundee, Scotland, where he studied illustration and printmaking, concentrating on book design in his postgraduate year. He has designed and created many new series of children's books for publishers in the U.K. and overseas.

Published in Great Britain by
Franklin Watts
96 Leonard Street
London
EC2A 4XD

Franklin Watts Australia
45-51 Huntley Street
Alexandria
NSW 2015

A CIP catalogue record for this book is available from the British Library

ISBN 0 7496 6220 4
Dewey classification 583

From Seed to Sunflower
Notes and activities by Karina Law, author and educational consultant

Each book in the *Lifecycles* series traces a story of growth and change.
Here are some ideas of how to get the most of *From Seed to Sunflower*:

Responding to the text

Once you have read through the book with children, ask open-ended questions to assess their comprehension.

• What happens when the tough seed-coat of the sunflower seed splits underground?

• How does the growing plant take in water from the soil?

• Why are insects attracted to flowers like the sunflower?

• How are seeds carried away from the sunflower to different places?

Features of non-fiction texts

Challenge children to locate specific information in the book using the contents page (page 6) or the index (page 29). Where would they look to find out about roots? Where could they find out about pollination? Which page would they turn to if they wanted to read about germination?

Look at other helpful features in the book, for example, labels and captions. How do these help the reader?

Look at the glossary of sunflower words on page 28. How many of these words were the children already familiar with? Which words are new to them? Why are the words in alphabetical order?

Language and literacy

Tell the story of Jack and the Beanstalk or, if the children are already familiar with the story, ask them to retell it to you. Ask them questions about the seeds and growth of the beanstalk. Could a beanstalk really grow that quickly? Why not? What type of seeds grow on beanstalks?

'Lifecycles' is a frequently studied topic with many cross-curricular links. Children can use *From Seed to Sunflower* as a starting point for looking at how other plants grow. Look at the plants in a garden or local park; how many of these have flowers? Which plants die away in the winter and which plants are evergreen? Think about edible plants that grow below ground, above ground and on trees and bushes.

lifecycles

From Seed to Sunflower

Written by Dr Gerald Legg
Illustrated by Carolyn Scrace

Created & Designed by David Salariya

W
FRANKLIN WATTS
LONDON•SYDNEY

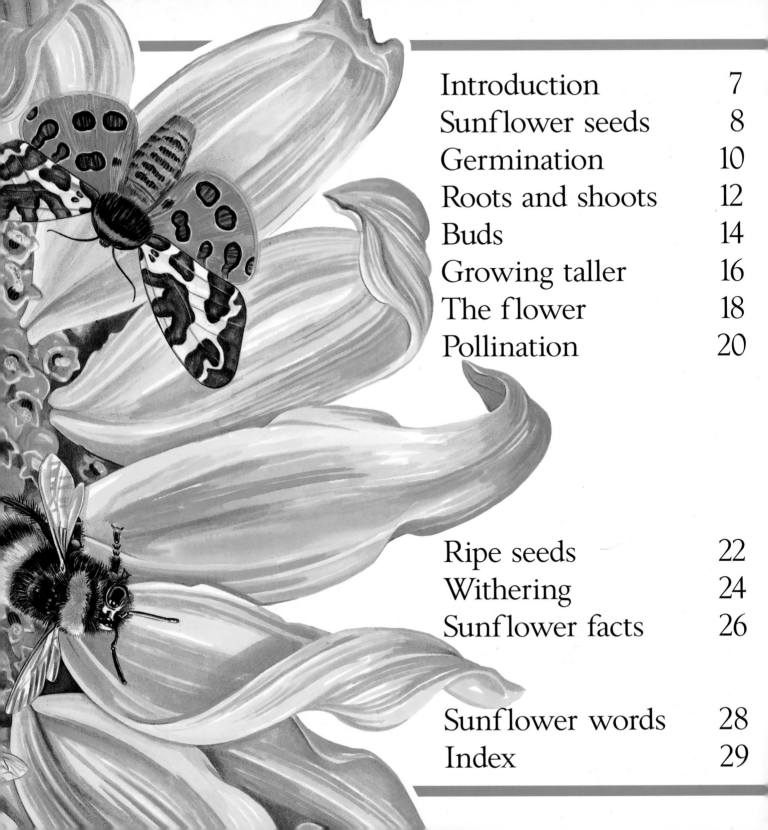

Plants use energy from the sun to make food. Minerals in the soil also help plants to grow. In this book you can see how a tiny seed grows into a beautiful sunflower.

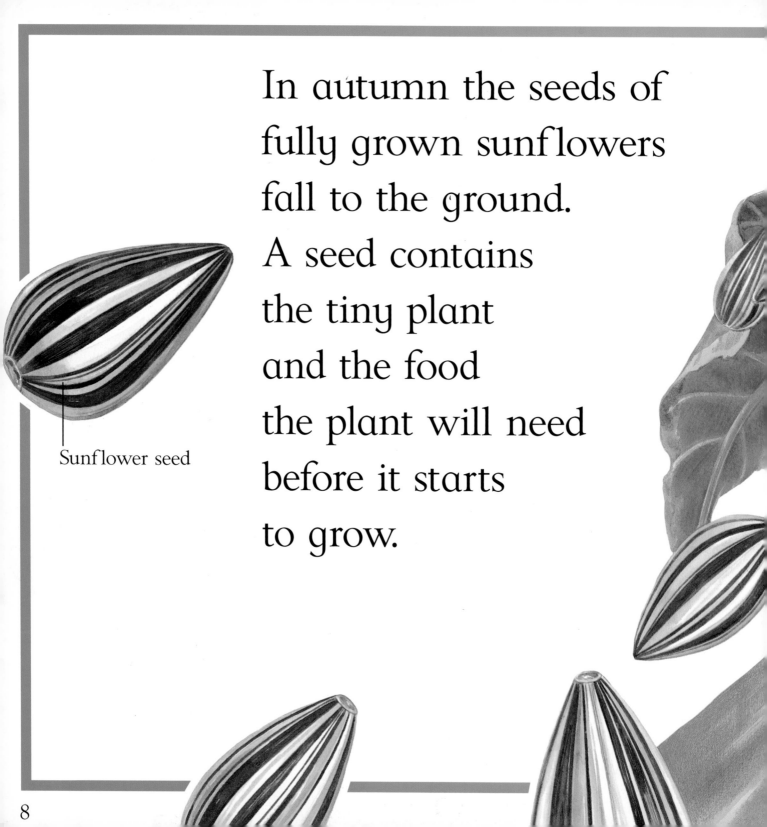

In autumn the seeds of
fully grown sunflowers
fall to the ground.
A seed contains
the tiny plant
and the food
the plant will need
before it starts
to grow.

Sunflower seed

8

The seeds are buried in the soil.
The soil contains minerals.
Minerals are special foods
that help the plant to grow.
In spring the warm sun and rain
make the seeds begin to grow.
This is called germination.

The seed lies
buried in the soil
all through
the winter.

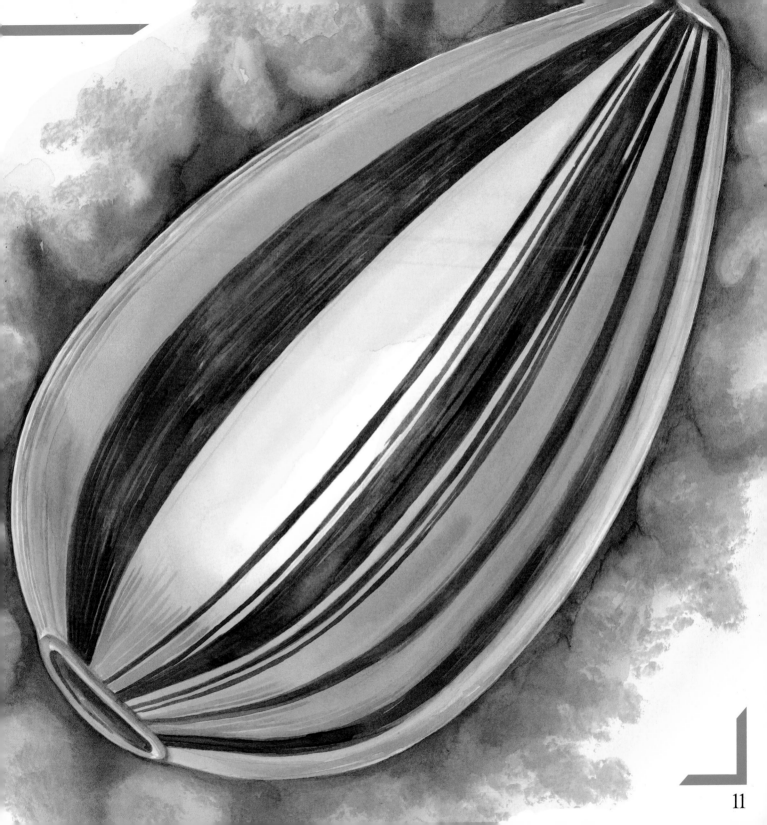

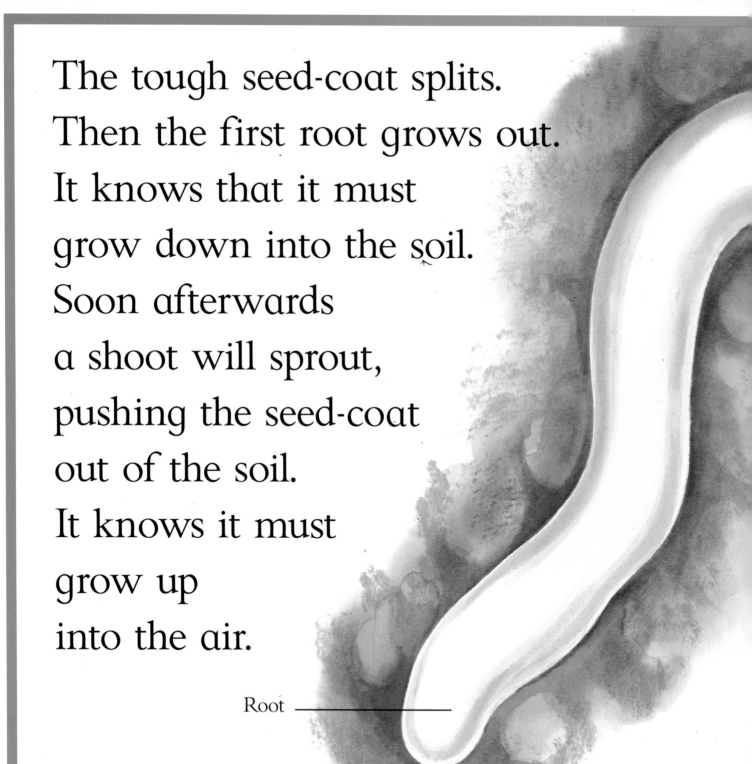

The tough seed-coat splits.
Then the first root grows out.
It knows that it must
grow down into the soil.
Soon afterwards
a shoot will sprout,
pushing the seed-coat
out of the soil.
It knows it must
grow up
into the air.

Root ————————————

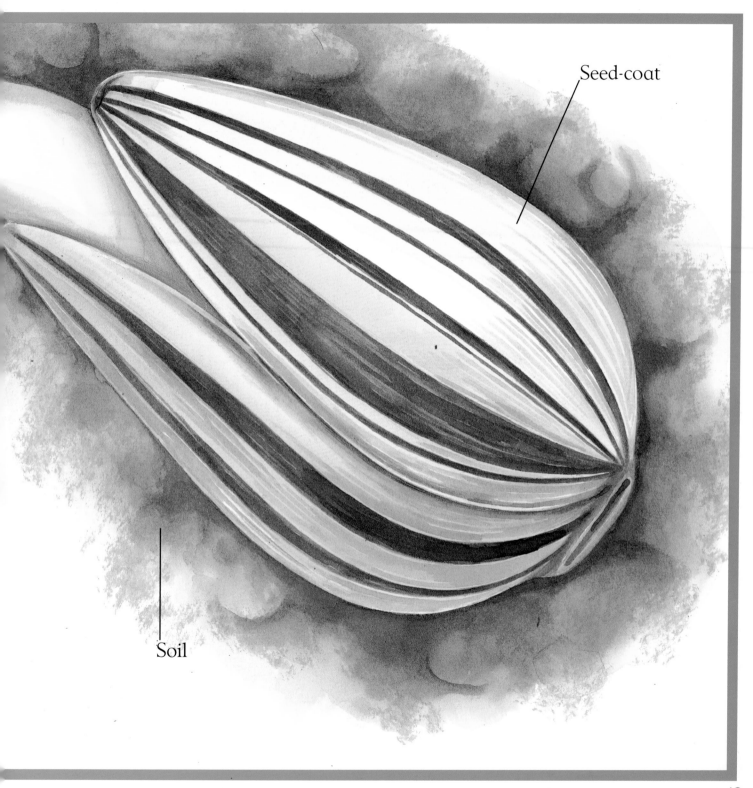
Seed-coat

Soil

13

Food stored inside the seed
helps the plant to grow.
Smaller roots begin to sprout
from the larger root.
The roots collect minerals
and water from the soil
to feed the growing plant.
A bud hidden between the
seed leaves pushes away
the split seed-coat.

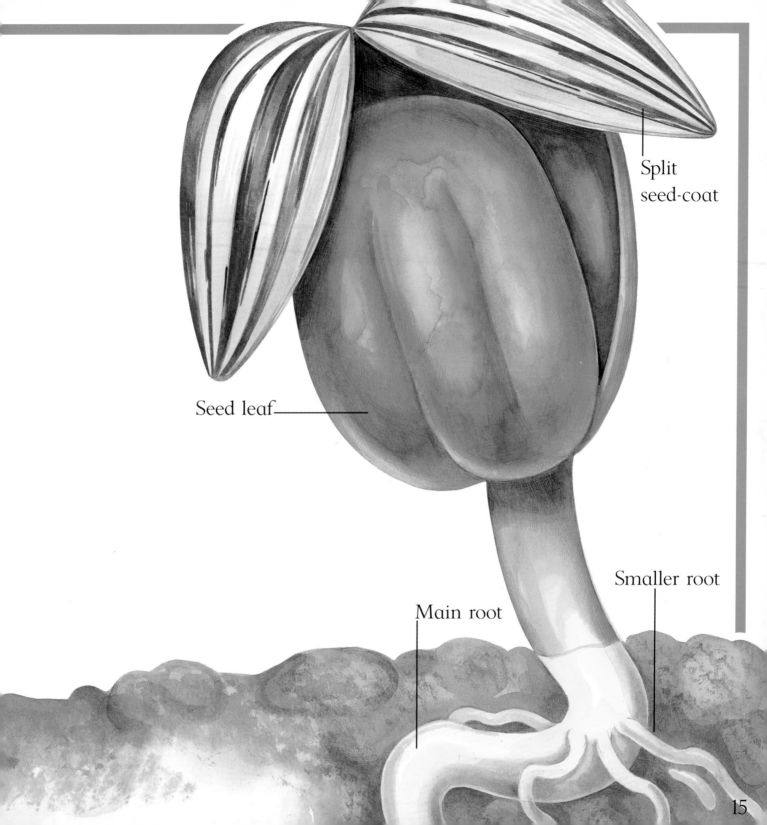

Split
seed-coat

Seed leaf

Main root

Smaller root

15

Ladybird

The young sunflower
grows taller and
more leaves sprout.
The leaves use air,
water and sunlight
to make food.
Flower buds form and
the roots grow longer.
The roots take in
water from the soil
and help to hold
the sunflower steady.

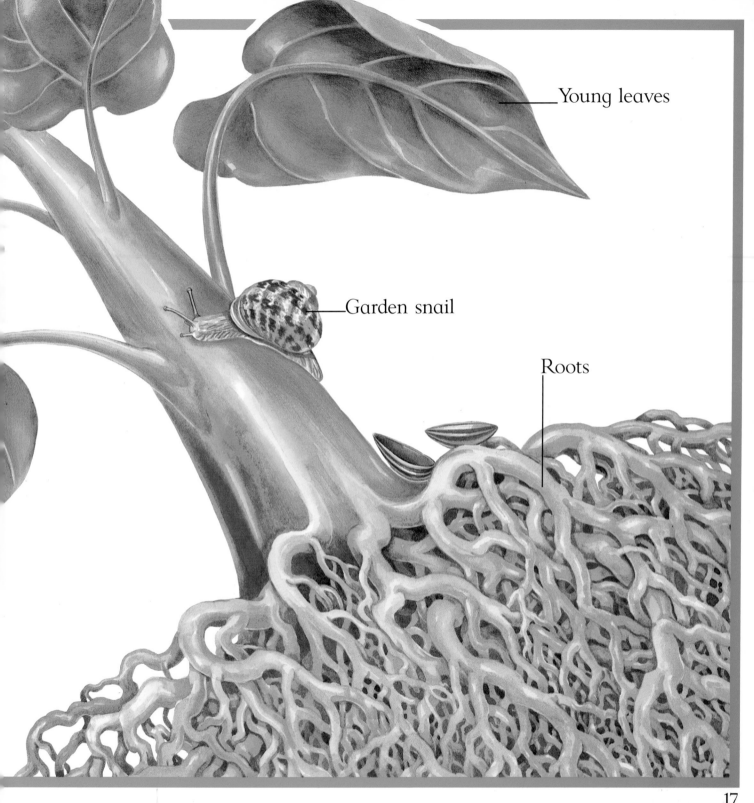

Young leaves

Garden snail

Roots

The flower bud grows
at the top of the stem.
Later it will open up
into a large flower head.
Each flower head is
made of lots of tiny flowers
packed together.
These tiny flowers
produce seeds.

Ladybird

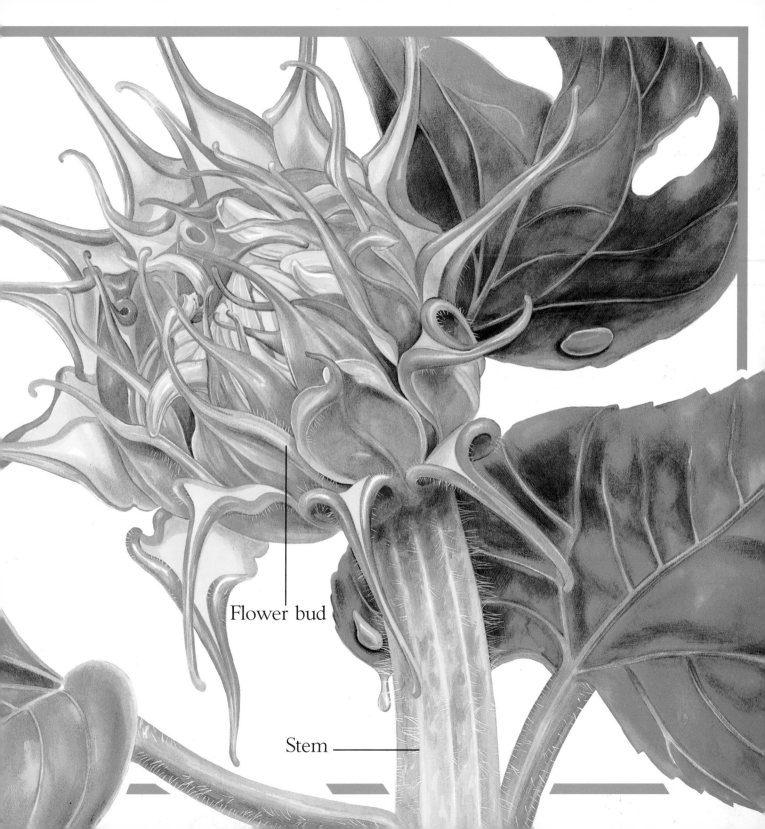

Flower bud

Stem

Insects are attracted to flowers
because flowers make
sweet nectar and pollen.
Insects drink nectar and,
as they fly between the plants,
they also carry
the sticky pollen
on the plants
from flower to flower.
It is the pollen that makes
plants produce new seeds.
This is called pollination.

The tiny seeds ripen.
Birds peck the seeds
in the flower heads.
Some seeds are eaten
and some are blown
away by the wind.
Some are caught in animal fur
and fall to the ground later.
Seeds can be carried far away
from the parent plant.

In autumn the
sunflower withers and dies.
The seeds that have not
been eaten or carried away
fall to the ground.
These seeds will be ready
to grow next spring.

The seeds fall
to the ground.

Withered flower head

Sunflower facts

Sunflower seeds are around 1 centimetre long.

The sunflower is a tall plant that can grow to 3.5 metres high.

The main root of the sunflower can grow 3 metres down into the ground.

The sunflower head can grow to around 40 centimetres across.

Some gardeners grow ornamental sunflowers with red, striped petals.

The main leaves of the sunflower are heart-shaped. They are around 30 centimetres across and 20 centimetres long.

The growth of a sunflower
In spring the seed-coat splits and the root and shoot sprout out. The root and the shoot use minerals from the soil to grow. The plant then buds and a sunflower grows. In autumn the sunflower withers and the seeds fall to the ground.

The sunflower turns its head towards the sun and follows it across the sky. In some countries it is called a sun-seeker.

Sunflowers were grown originally by Native Americans, from southern Canada to Mexico.

Sunflower seeds were brought over from America to Spain in 1510.

Seed   The seed leaves sprout.   5 weeks   9 weeks

Around 200 years ago farmers started to grow sunflowers so that the seeds could be crushed to make sunflower oil.

America is the main grower of sunflowers, but they are also grown in Europe.

Oil from the seeds is used for cooking. The seeds themselves can be eaten, too.

The remains of the crushed seeds can be used as animal feed.

Budding   12 weeks   Flowering   Fully grown   Withering   Falling seeds

Sunflower words

Bud
The top of a shoot or branch. New leaves and flowers grow inside the bud.

Extinct
A plant or animal that has died out forever.

Germination
The stage in the life cycle of a plant when the seeds first begin to grow.

Minerals
Special food in the soil. Plants need minerals to help them grow.

Nectar
Sweet, sugary liquid made by flowers to attract insects.

Pollen
The fine dust of a male flower. Insects and wind transfer pollen to the female plant. When this happens seeds are made.

Pollination
The movement of pollen from one flower to another.

Root
The part of a plant that grows down into the soil.

Seed
The part of the plant that contains the young plant. When it grows the young plant appears.

Seed-coat
The tough outer layer of a seed.

Seed leaves
The very first leaves that a plant grows when it grows from the seed.

Shoot
The young branch or stem of a plant.

Stem
The part of the plant that grows up into the air. Flowers and leaves grow from the stem.

Wither
To dry up.

Index

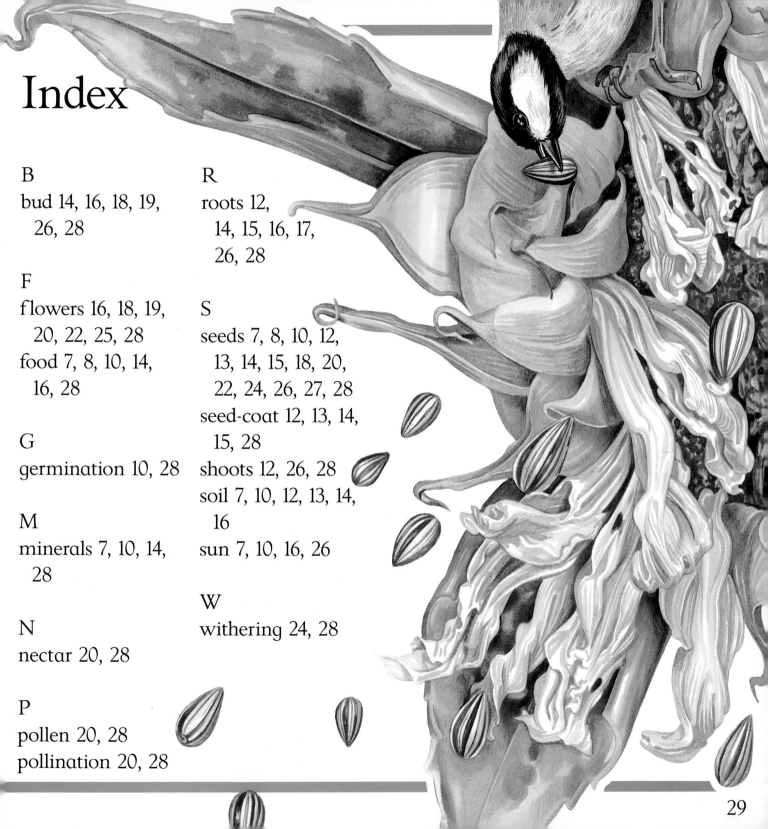